YOUR KNOWLEDGE HAS VALUE

Bibliographic information published by the German National Library:

The German National Library lists this publication in the National Bibliography; detailed bibliographic data are available on the Internet at http://dnb.dnb.de .

Imprint:

Copyright © 2012 GRIN Verlag
Print and binding: Books on Demand GmbH, Norderstedt Germany
ISBN: 9783668838611

Dileep Keshava Narayana

IT Application Security and Control

GRIN Verlag

GRIN - Your knowledge has value

Since its foundation in 1998, GRIN has specialized in publishing academic texts by students, college teachers and other academics as e-book and printed book. The website www.grin.com is an ideal platform for presenting term papers, final papers, scientific essays, dissertations and specialist books.

Visit us on the internet:

http://www.grin.com/

http://www.facebook.com/grincom

http://www.twitter.com/grin_com

CONTENTS

1. Part 1   2

    1.1 Weekly assignment: Steganography exercise   2

    1.2 Weekly assignment: Digital Watermarking exercise   4

    1.3 Churchill secondary school data protection report   5

    1.4 Final Report   8

2. Part 2   9

    2.1 Lab: Database Authentication   9

    2.2 Lab: Database Authorization: Privileges and role based security   13

    2.3 Lab: Database Authorization and data integrity (Views, Constraints)   18

    2.4 Lab: Implementing Virtual private database   27

    2.5 Churchill secondary school database security policy   36

        2.5.1   Database Security Policy   36

        2.5.2   Database Security policy implementation   37

        2.5.3   Final Report   40

        References   41

PART 1

1.1 Weekly Assignment: Steganography exercise

To,

Mr. Wickchad

Managing Director

Wickchad Motors

Subject: - Advise on the use of steganography for inter-branch email communication.

Dear Mr.Wickchad,

I have analysed the proposed method for the use of steganography for inter-branch email communication. I am including the details of my analysis below in detail.

The proposed picture consists of 8m pixels.

So 8m pixels = 8000000 pixels

Picture uses 2 bytes to define colour of each pixel. So it is 16 bit grayscale image.

Sampling factor = 0.5

Expected result:

Can hide 400 pages of A4 text

1 word = 5 characters (Including Space).

A4 page = 50 lines.

1 line = 10 words.

After the detailed analysis of the proposed method, I saw that the expected result does not match the actual results. Below I am including the actual results with calculation and explanation.

Calculation of size of the digital picture:

1 MB = 1024 KB

1 KB = 1024 bytes

1 byte = 8 bits

Bit Depth = 8 * 2 = 16 bit

Colour Depth = 2^{16} = 65536 colours

Size = Number of Pixels * Number of bits used to store a pixel

File Size = 8000000 * 2 bytes = 16000000 bytes = 15.25 MB

Variation of colour in each pixel

Each pixel consists of 2 bytes. So 2 bytes = 16 bit.

For 16 bit colour depth is 2^{16} = 65536 colours.

Therefore each pixel can be defined to have 65536 colour variations.

Number of characters of data that can be hidden in picture

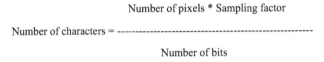

$$\text{Number of characters} = \frac{\text{Number of pixels * Sampling factor}}{\text{Number of bits}}$$

$$= \frac{8000000 * 0.5}{8 * 2} = 250000 \text{ Characters}$$

Actual Result

We can hide 100 pages of A4 text.

50000 Words

5000 lines

Conclusion: There is a miscalculation in the proposed method of DataSec plc as shown above the expected results does not meet the actual results.

The correct figure of number of A4 pages of text can be hidden is 100.

Advantages of the proposed method by DataSec plc

The proposed method of DataSec plc has advantages such as we can hide 100 pages of A4 text which is beneficial for shorter communications.

Disadvantages of the proposed method by DataSec plc

The proposed method can be intercepted easily and it is less secure.

Suggestions: I suggest for keeping email communication among inter-branches more secure, we should use the 32 bit or higher bit depth which provides 2^{32} colours variation in each pixel and that makes it difficult to intercept the communication. This provides the secure communication among inter-branches and we can even increase the hiding capability which suites longer conversations.

Regards

-Dileep

Security Consultant

WickChad motors.

1.2 Weekly Assignment: Digital watermarking exercise

4m pixels = 4000000 pixels

Two bytes to define colour of each pixel.

a) Each character is stored in 1 byte.

Phrase = thisphotoisthecopyrightofphotographerdavidchadwick = 50 characters.

To hide this 50 characters phrase we need 400 bits.

i.e. For 8 bits ---------- 1 character can be hidden

?   ------------- 50 character to be hidden

50 * 8 = 400 bits.

b) 20 identical phrases as a) are to be stored in the photograph as watermark.

So 20 * 50 = 1000 characters.

To store 1000 characters we need 8000 bits.

As for every 8 bit 1 character is hidden, bit depth is 16 bit as it uses 2 bytes to store colour.

Therefore sampling factor can be calculated as numbers of bits/total bits in picture.

Total bits in picture = 16 * 4000000.

Number of bits including 20 phrases = 800 bits

Sampling factor = 8000/64000000 = 0.000125

Higher the sampling factor weaker the approach. So the sampling factor for this approach is small. This approach is good and is stronger.

Approach is stronger as there is a large of amount space to hide the 20 phrases and it is difficult to know the digits altered.

c) Pic Scout Image tracker protects the images of the image owner by licensing it. Pic Scout Image Tracker can be used to license the images on web for the creative professional with image information. It allows to select the finest quality images and to improve the satisfaction of the clients.

It also allows the image owners to distribute the picture safely on web by licensing it. The image licensors can track where the images reside in web and are being used.

d) The program should be designed in such a way that it searches all the pixel bits with the lower case alphabets ASCII code. The pixel bit which matches the lower case alphabets ASCII code can be detected. And then the default value values of RGB colours which are not matched in each pixel might contain the watermarking. By detecting these areas we can further proceed to detect where the watermark is hidden. By editing these areas by the default value of RGB colour we can remove the watermarking.

We can remove the hidden watermarks by clone tool by selecting the bits to copy to the image. However for this first we need to first detect the bits where the watermark is hidden. And then the missing bit must be filled with the appropriate colour bits.

Now a days we can remove the visible watermark by using the spot healing tool provided by the softwares such as Photoshop, creativity suite and others.

1.3 Churchill secondary school Data protection report

School

Data protection report for Churchill school is as follows:

1) Data must be held for specifically for the specified and lawful purpose and not processed in anyway incompatible with those purposes.

2) Data must be obtained and processed, fairly and lawfully.

3) Data must not be kept no longer than necessary for stated purpose.

4) Data must be accurate and up-to-date.

5) Data must be processed with respect to the rights of datasubjects.

6) Appropriate technical/ Organizational measures to be taken against loss/unauthorized disclosure/ corruption of data.

Head and vice head teacher:

Head and vice head teacher have full access to the data. As Head and vice head teacher are the authorized personnels, the data must be encrypted by using encryption techniques such as symmetric encryption and digital signatures.

In education the student personal details must be kept for a limited time and the information must be synchronized to the UK data controller.

The following data protection act applies to Head and vice head teacher of the Churchill secondary school for the usage of data:

1) Must be held only for educational purpose only and not processed in any way incompatible with this purpose.

   The student details must be held for the educational purpose only. The details must not be provided to any other purposes such as marketing etc.

2) Must be processed with respect to the rights of data subjects.

   Data must be accessed only when it is necessary to access it and upon the request only.

3) Must be obtained and processed, fairly and lawfully.

   Details of the staff's must be obtained, processed fairly and as per the UK government educational institution laws.

4) Must be accurate, relevant, and not excessive for purpose.

   Staff such as teachers must be provided limited access such as limiting to view the student details of his/her engaging class only.

   Teaching assistants must only have read-only access to teaching materials to which teacher they are allocated.

   In the same way for other staffs.

5) Must be accurate and up-to-date.

   The staff and students data such as personal details, qualifications, marks obtained must be accurate and up-to-date. Head and vice head teacher must not provide false information about the staff for the UK government.

6) Should not be transferred to a country or territory outside the European economic area.

   The student details and staff details must not be transferred to other countries. At some case upon the request from the authorized personnel for the verification of the student or by the employer the details of the student or staff can be provided for the further education or for the employment purpose only, however personal details must not be provided without the without authorization for any other purpose.

7) Appropriate school measures to be taken against the loss/ unauthorized disclosure/ corruption of data.

   If any of the staff discloses the data or losses the data or corrupts the data appropriate measures must be taken such as compensating for the damage, or handing the staff to police.

Teachers:

Teachers must have full access to all teaching materials and pupil's profile for the class which they are managing or handling.

The following data protection act applies to the teachers of the Churchill secondary school for the usage of data:

1) Must be obtained and processed, fairly and lawfully.

   Teachers must obtain the data of the students only when it is necessary and/or upon request from parents or students only or to review the performance of the students or to improve the performance only,

2) Must be processed with respect to the rights of data subjects.

   Teachers must only use the teaching materials for educational purpose in school only.

3) Must be kept no longer than necessary for the educational purpose.

   When they are not handling a class they must not use the same details for any other purpose.

4) Must not be transferred to a country or territory outside the European economic area.

   Personal details of the students must not be disclosed to anyone, except to student's parents upon specific authorization.

Teaching assistant:

Teaching assistant must only have read only access to teaching materials from the teacher they are assigned to.

The following data protection act applies for the Teaching assistants in Churchill secondary school.

1) Must be obtained and processed, fairly and lawfully.

   Teaching assistants must only view the teaching materials allocated to them only for the teaching purpose.

2) Must be processed with respect to the rights of data subjects

Educational psychologist:

Educational psychologist must have full access to pupil's personal profiles such as their marks obtained, age and the like.

The following data protection acts is applicable for educational psychologists in Churchill secondary school:

1) Must be processed with respect to the rights of data subjects.

Educational psychologists must only use the data to obtain the information about the students for advising them to improve their performance.

2) Must be held only for specified and lawful purposes and not processed in any way incompatible with those purposes.

Educational psychologist must only use the information of the students to advise the students to improve the problems by knowing the cause of the problem.

Administration staff:

Administrative staff must have read only access to the financial and administrative data only.

The following data protection act applies to Members of administration in Churchill secondary school:

1) Must be processed with respect to the rights of data subjects.

Members of administration only deal with finance and administrative data, anything beyond that must not be collected with the students or the relatives of the students.

2) Must be accurate and up-to-date.

Members of administration must update the finance and administrative data correctly without any mistake.

3) Must be obtained and processed, fairly and lawfully.

If student pays the fees then it must be obtained, processed fairly and lawfully by providing the receipt of it.

1.4 Final Report (Conclusion)

IT Application security plays an important role in maintaining the security of the data or information in all kinds of organization. Confidentiality, Authenticity, and Integrity of the data is important in all the organization.

In this Part1 Coursework, we learnt how to make the communication of the organization more secure with their inter-branches by using steganography. We analysed and evaluated the proposed approach whether the expected result matches the actual calculation results. Unfortunately, it didn't match the actual results so advise has been made to make the approach better to the managing director of Wickchad motors by writing a letter.

Next, we also learnt about digital watermarking. Hiding the watermark in the image, tool used to make it and to detect the image on web where it resides.

Finally, Data protection policy has been created for the Churchill secondary school and for the staffs of the school by taking the legal laws into consideration.

PART 2

2.1 LAB: Database Authentication

2.1.1 Overview

In this laboratory project we explored the different aspects of the database authentication as well as the use of the user accounts and password controls.
By this lab, we will be able to

- Use the data dictionary to find information about users and security information
- Create new user accounts
- Determine password limits for database users
- Create and assign profiles

Lab 2.1.2: Exploring data dictionary

a) **Open SQL*Plus window and connect using your yoda account, that was tested last week.**

We can connect to the yoda database by using the command:

connect username/password@databasename;

Ex: *connect kd105/kd105@yoda;*

It must say connected once the command is entered if the username, password and database name is correct.

b) **Find out how many objects in the data dictionary hold information about users; write downs the number.**

To find how many objects in the data dictionary hold the information about users, you can use the following SQL command:

```
select * from dictionary where table_name like '%USERS%';
```

Question1: How many objects in the data dictionary hold information about users?

There are six Objects in the data dictionary which holds information about users as given below.

DBA_USERS   V$PWFILE_USERS

ALL_USERS   GV$PWFILE_USERS

USER_USERS

DBA_USERS_WITH_DEFPWD

c) **Investigate what information can you get from the table USER_USERS about each user?**

The information can be got by using:
desc USER_USERS;

Question 2: What information about each user can you derive from the table USER_USERS?

We can derive the information like *Username, User id, Account Status, Lock date, Expiry date, Default Tablespace, Temporary Tablespace, Created, Initial resource consumer group of the each user* and *datatypes.*

d) **Find out all details of your account from the USER_USERS.**

The details of the account can be found out by using the command:

select * from USER_USERS where username= 'KD105';

e) **Question 3: Can you see password in USER_USERS table? Explain.**

No, we cannot see the password in the USER_USERS table because the passwords are stored encrypted in the data dictionary which cannot be decrypted other than the oracle database engine.

Lab 2.1.3: Creating a new user

1) **You need to create a new user in yoda database.**

CREATE USER kd105_a IDENTIFIED BY connect1;

a) **Create a new user with following information Username=xxxx_A (Where xxxx is your yoda username), Password=connect1 (password is case sensitive)**

The new user can be created by using the command:
CREATE USER kd105_a IDENTIFIED BY connect1;

b) **Connect to SQL*Plus as a new user**

To connect to the new user following command is used:
Connect kd105_a/connect1@yoda;

c) **Question 4: What is the result? Write down the error and explain.**

The error is "ORA-01045: User kd105_a lacks the CREATE SESSION privilege; login denied".

We created the user successfully but we did not grant the session for the new user. Until and unless the session is granted the user cannot login.

d)   Connect to SQL*Plus as your original username using following:

To connect to SQL*Plus following command is used:

Connect kd105/kd105@yoda;

e)   Grant CREATE *SESSION* privilege to a new user.

GRANT CREATE SESSION to kd105_A;

f)   Now try to connect as new user

CONNECT kd105_A/connect1@yoda;

g)   Question 5. What is the result? Explain.

As we granted the session for the new user now the result is "Connected".

Lab 2.1.4: Creating and using profile

1) Create a new profile

a)   Connect to SQL*Plus as your original username

By using the following command we can connect to the original username:

CONNECT kd105/kd105@yoda;

b)   Create a profile

Profile can be created by using the following command:

CREATE PROFILE kd105_prof

LIMIT FAILED_LOGIN_ATTEMPTS 2

PASSWORD_LOCK_TIME 1

PASSWORD_LIFE_TIME 180

PASSWORD_REUSE_TIME 2

PASSWORD_REUSE_MAX UNLIMITED;

c)   Assign new profile to your new user

To assign new profile to the new user following command is used.

ALTER USER kd105_A PROFILE kd105_prof;

2) Test the security features, provided by a new profile

a)   Connect as xxxx_A user, but provide a wrong password

CONNECT kd105_A/kd125@yoda;

b) Try 2 times.

Need to enter the wrong password 2 times.

c) Question 6: What is the result? Explain.

The result is the error "the Account is locked".

As the *LIMIT FAILED_LOGIN_ATTEMPTS* is 2 in the profile, so it can only accepts the two failed login attempts to the account and then the account is locked.

3) Unlock xxxx_A account

a) Connect as your original yoda user and unlock the xxxx_A user account:

CONNECT kd105/kd105@yoda;

To unlock the account use the following command:

ALTER USER kd105_A ACCOUNT UNLOCK;

4) Check how many times you can re-use the same password:

a) Connect as a xxxx_A user

CONNECT kd105_A/connect1@yoda;

b) Change the password using following command:

ALTER USER kd105_A identified by connect1;

c) Try to it again:

ALTER USER xxxx_A identified by connect1;

d) Question 7: Explain the result.

As *PASSWORD_REUSE_TIME* is *2* in profile, after the 2 attempt of reusing the same password, it says "the password cannot be reused" and we need to provide a different password.

2.2 LAB: Database Authorization: Privileges and role-based security

2.2.1 Overview

In this laboratory project we will explore the different aspects of the database authorisation, particularly use of system and object privileges as well as roles. At the end of this project, we will be able to

- Use the data dictionary to find information about user privileges
- Assign system and object privileges to users
- Create roles and assign them to users
- Test database authorisation

Note: - In this whole lab exercise kd105, kd105_A, kd105_B is username, kd105, connect1, connect2 is password respectively, yoda is the database name, and kd105_clerk is the role.

Lab 2.2.2: Connect as your original yoda user and create a new table.

1) Open SQL*Plus window and connect to yoda database.

To connect for yoda database first open the sql plus and type the command below is used:
connect kd105/kd105@yoda;

This connects to yoda database.

2) Create a table *bonus* as following:
   CREATE TABLE bonus (id NUMBER, category VARCHAR2(20), amount NUMBER);

This will create the table *bonus* with *id, category* and *amount* as the columns.

Question1: What privilege do you need to have in order to create new table? Is it a system or object privilege?

We need to have the *create table* privilege in order to create new table. In order to create table in user's table we need to have *create any table* privilege. *Create table, Create any table are* system privilege.

3) Insert a few records into this table and commit:

The records are inserted into the *bonus* table *as* shown below:
INSERT INTO bonus VALUES (1, 'CLERK', 100);
INSERT INTO bonus VALUES (2, 'MANAGER', 300);
INSERT INTO bonus VALUES (3, 'VP', 500);
COMMIT;

This will insert the 4 records into the *bonus* table.

4) Check if you can see these records

To check the records following command is used:
*SELECT * FROM bonus;*

Lab 2.2.3: Granting privileges to a new user.

1) In the lab 2 we have created a new user *kd105_A*

If we need to create the new user, we can do it by using the command:
CREATE USER kd105_A IDENTIFIED BY connect1;
We can grant session for the new user by using the command:
GRANT CREATE SESSION TO kd105_A;

This will grant session for user.

a) Grant user *kd105_A* a permission (privilege) to view your table bonus:

To grant the user *kd105_A* the privilege to access table bonus we use the following command:
GRANT SELECT ON bonus TO kd105_A;

b) Connect to SQL*Plus as a new user using following:

To connect to SQL*plus to the user *kd105_A* we use:
CONNECT kd105_A/connect1@yoda;

c) Query new table using *SELECT * FROM bonus;*

Question 2: What is the result? Please provide detailed explanation.

The result is *"Error ORA-00942: Table or view does not exist"*.

It says error because kd105 is the owner of the bonus table. It can only be accessed by using the command as shown below:

*SELECT * FROM kd105.bonus;*

d) Correct your query:

To view the table bonus use the following command:
*SELECT * FROM kd105.bonus;*

e) Try to update one of the records in the kd105.bonus table:

To update the records we use the command given below:

UPDATE kd105.bonus SET amount=600 WHERE id =3;

Question3: What is the result? Please provide detailed explanation.

We will get *"Error ORA-01031: Insufficient privileges"*. As we just grant the privilege to only view the table and didn't grant the permission to update the table.

Question4: What privilege(s) you need to have in order to be able to insert, update and delete records from the table kd105.bonus?

We need to have the create table privilege to insert, update and delete the table to insert, update and delete records for the users kd105_A and kd105_B to pursue the task.

14

Lab 2.2.4: Create a second user and grant necessary privileges.

1) Connect to SQL*Plus as your original yoda user (xxxxx)

2) Now you need to create another user kd105_B

  a) CREATE USER kd105_B IDENTIFIED BY connect2;

  b) Grant this user Create Session privilege:

    GRANT CREATE SESSION TO kd105_B;

3) Now you decided to grant both users *kd105_A* and *kd105_B* a full access to your table *bonus*.

To grant both users *kd105_A* and *kd105_B* full access to the table *bonus* we use following commands:

GRANT CREATE SESSION TO kd105_A;

GRANT CREATE SESSION TO kd105_B;

Question 5: What is best way to achieve this task? Provide detailed explanation.

We can provide just *create session* privilege to multiple users by using command below:

GRANT CREATE SESSION TO kd105_A, kd105_B;

In general we can use

GRANT CREATE SESSION TO username1, username2, username3...;

And if we can also provide multiple privileges to multiple users at the same time by using the command:

GRANT CREATE SESSION, CREATE TABLE TO username1, username2...;

The best way of managing privileges is by using roles. We can create roles which are named as the groups of related privileges.

  a) Create new role with the name *kd105_clerk.*

    We can create new role by using the command below:

    CREATE ROLE kd105_clerk;

  b) Grant this role necessary privileges:

    We can grant all the necessary privilege for bonus table for the role by using:

    GRANT ALL on bonus to kd105_clerk;

  c) Assign this role to both users kd105_A and kd105_B:

    We can assign the role kd105_clerk to the users kd105_A and kd105_b by using:

    GRANT kd105_clerk to kd105_A, kd105_B;

  d) Test both users A and B:

    To test both the users kd105_A and kd105_B whether the permission is granted

First Connect as *kd105_A* user. Try to update any record in the kd105.bonus table.
To connect to kd105_A user use

CONNECT kd105_A/connect1@yoda;

Now update the record by using the command as below:

UPDATE kd105.bonus SET amount=400 WHERE id=2;

Result of this would be '1 row updated'.

Now Connect as kd105_B user and try to select records from kd105.bonus table.
To connect to kd105_B user use:

CONNECT kd105_B/connect2@yoda;

Now to select the recrods from kd105.bonus table use the following:

*SELECT * FROM kd105.bonus;*

We will get the table with the amount updated for the id-2.

Question6: Can the users A and update records in kd105.bonus table? Explain.

Yes, both the users kd105_A and kd105_B can update the records in kd105.bonus table. As
We have assigned the role of clerk to both kd105_A and kd105_B.

Lab 2.2.5: Revoking privileges.

1) Connect to SQL*Plus as your original yoda user (kd105).

To connect to user kd105 use the following:

CONNECT kd105/kd105@yoda;

2) Revoke the privilege to update bonus table from kd105_A user

  To remove the permission of update on the bonus table which was previously
allocated for the user kd105_A use the following:

REVOKE SELECT ON bonus FROM kd105_A;

3) Test kd105_A user:

Connect as kd105_A user and try to select records from kd105.bonus table.
To connect to user kd105_A use:

CONNECT kd105_A/connect1@yoda;

To select records from kd105.bonus use:

*SELECT * FROM kd105.bonus;*

Question7: What is the result? Explain.

Even though we revoked the select on bonus privilege from kd105_A still there is privilege for this user, as has been granted the role of clerk which has the full access privilege on the *bonus* table.

3) Test kd105_B user: try to select records from kd105.bonus table.

Connect as kd105_B user and try to select records from kd105.bonus table.

To connect to kd105_B use:

CONNECT kd105_B/connect2@yoda;

To select records from kd105.bonus use:

*SELECT * FROM kd105_B.bonus;*

Question8: What is the result? Explain.

The user kd105_B can access and select records from kd105.bonus table because it has been granted the full access privilege in the role of clerk.

Question9: What is best way to revoke all privileges from both users? Write down the command but don't execute it.

To remove all the privileges from both users kd105_A and kd105_B we need to remove the role of the clerk from them by using the following:

REVOKE kd105_clerk FROM kd105_A, kd105_B;

To remove all the privileges for both users we can use:

REVOKE ALL FROM kd105_A, kd105_B;

Question10: How to find out all privileges assigned to a particular role? Use the lecture material and write and execute SQL statement that shows all privileges assigned to a role *clerk*. Provide screen-shot of the result.

We can find the permissions assigned to the role by checking in the data dictionary items ROLE_SYS_PRIVS for system privileges and ROLE_TAB_PRIVS for object privileges

We can use the following commands to pursue this task:

*SELECT * FROM ROLE_SYS_PRIVS WHERE ROLE= 'kd105_clerk;*

*SELECT * FROM ROLE_TAB_PRIVS WHERE ROLE= 'kd105.clerk;*

2.3 LAB: Database Authorization & Data integrity (views, constraints)

Lab 2.3.1: Implementing integrity constraints.

1) You need to create two tables according to the following requirements:

Table: **Lab4Department**

Table columns description:

1. dept_no , Number type, must be a primary key for the Lab4Department table.

2. dept_name, Varchar2 type, maximum length 30, cannot contain NULL values.

3. location Varchar2 type, maximum length 25.

Table: **Lab4Student**

Table Columns:

1. student_id , Number type, must be a primary key for the Lab4Student table.

2. first_name, Varchar2 type, maximum length 30, cannot contain NULL values.

3. last_name, Varchar2 type, maximum length 30, cannot contain NULL values.

4. gender, Varchar2 type, maximum length 1, cannot contain any other values except

   M and F.

5. student_dept, Number type, must reference dept_no column in Lab4Department table.

2) Test your new tables.

a) Insert first record into Lab4Department table. Commit.

b) Try to insert the second record into Lab4Department table with exact the same dept_no.

c) Insert first record into Lab4Student table. Commit.

d) Try to insert a record into Lab4Student table where student_dept number doesn't match dept_no in Lab4Department table.

e) Try to insert a record into Lab4Student table with the value 'Male' for the gender column.

Question1: Provide the complete SQL commands for the creation of the *Lab4Department* table and the *Lab4Student* table as well as the screen shots of the test results.

Create table lab4department(dept_no number, dept_name varchar2(30) not null, location varchar2(25), constraint pk_dno primary key(dept_no));

```
Oracle SQL*Plus
File  Edit  Search  Options  Help
SQL>
SQL> create table lab4department(dept_no number,dept_name varchar2(30) not null,
  2  location varchar2(25),constraint pk_dno primary key(dept_no));

Table created.
```

Create table lab4student(student_id number, first_name varchar2(30) not null, last_name varchar2(30) not null, gender varchar2(1) , constraint pk_sid primary key(student_id), student_dept number, constraint fk_dname foreign key(student_dept) references lab4department(dept_no), constraint gen check(gender in('M', 'F')));

```
Oracle SQL*Plus
File  Edit  Search  Options  Help
SQL>
SQL> create table lab4student(student_id number,first_name varchar2(30) not null,
  2  last_name varchar2(30) not null,gender varchar2(1),
  3  constraint pk_sid primary key(student_id),student_dept number,
  4  constraint fk_dname foreign key(student_dept) references lab4department(dept_no)
  5  ,constraint gen check(gender in('M','F')));

Table created.
```

2) Test your new tables.

a) Insert first record into Lab4Department table. Commit

```
Oracle SQL*Plus
File  Edit  Search  Options  Help
SQL>
SQL> insert into lab4department values
  2  (10,'cse','london');

1 row created.

SQL> commit;

Commit complete.
```

b) Try to insert the second record into Lab4Department table with exact the same dept_no.

```
Oracle SQL*Plus
File   Edit   Search   Options   Help
SQL>
SQL> insert into lab4department values
  2  (10,'csit','kent');
insert into lab4department values
*
ERROR at line 1:
ORA-00001: unique constraint (CU020.PK_DNO) violated
```

c) Insert first record into Lab4Student table. Commit.

```
Oracle SQL*Plus
File   Edit   Search   Options   Help

SQL> insert into lab4student values
  2  (1,'mitch','gaylord','M',10);

1 row created.

SQL> commit;

Commit complete.
```

d) Try to insert a record into Lab4Student table where student_dept number doesn't match dept_no in Lab4Department table.

```
Oracle SQL*Plus
File  Edit  Search  Options  Help
SQL>
SQL> insert into lab4student values
  2  (2,'leverock','douglas','M',20);
insert into lab4student values
*
ERROR at line 1:
ORA-02291: integrity constraint (CU020.FK_DNAME) violated - parent key not
found
```

e) Try to insert a record into Lab4Student table with the value 'Male' for the gender column.

```
Oracle SQL*Plus
File   Edit   Search   Options   Help
SQL>
SQL> insert into lab4student values
  2  (2,'john','reed','Male',10);
(2,'john','reed','Male',10)
             *
ERROR at line 2:
ORA-12899: value too large for column "CU020"."LAB4STUDENT"."GENDER" (actual:
4, maximum: 1)
```

Lab 2.3.2: Creating views
Lab4.2.1: Create a view that is hiding sensitive information (NHS number) in the PATIENT table.

1) Investigate data in the PATIENT table:

*SELECT * FROM gp.patient;*

```
Oracle SQL*Plus

File  Edit  Search  Options  Help

SQL> select * from gp.patient;

NHS_NO          SURNAME                 FORENAMES                        G DATE_OF_B
--------------  ----------------------  -------------------------------  - ---------
FAMQ221         Gloria                  Heyward                          F 12-OCT-43
MSAK222         Ian                     Allen                            M 29-FEB-64
MDAQ123         Mel                     Andrews                          M 17-MAR-37
FEAW224         Ntina                   Antoniou                         F 21-MAR-54
FFAQ225         Audrey                  Garland                          F 12-APR-50
FCAD126         Yolanda                 Baly                             F 25-JAN-39
FSAQ327         Joanna                  Bennett                          F 09-JAN-48
MRAQ228         Mohand                  Bougan                           M 20-JAN-65
FTAD429         Pat                     Brady                            F 01-FEB-59
FGAC520         Dianne                  Bullman                          F 27-APR-55
MHAU621         Jonathan                Branwell                         M 14-MAY-56

NHS_NO          SURNAME                 FORENAMES                        G DATE_OF_B
--------------  ----------------------  -------------------------------  - ---------
MBAF722         Steve                   Husson                           M 12-JUN-66
MBAR823         David                   Bullman                          M 29-MAR-53
```

2) You need to create a view based on the PATIENT table, which displays all information from this table except the patient's NHS number.

Complete the following SQL command and execute it.
CREATE OR REPLACE VIEW patient_info AS

SELECT ....

FROM gp.patient;

3) Test your new view

*SELECT * FROM patient_info;*

Question2: Provide the complete SQL command for the *patient_info* view and the screen shot of the test result.

CREATE OR REPLACE VIEW patient_info AS

SELECT SURNAME,FORENAMES,GENDER,DATE_OF_BIRTH

FROM gp.patient;

```
Oracle SQL*Plus
File  Edit  Search  Options  Help

SQL> create or replace view patient_info as
  2    select surname,forenames,gender,date_of_birth
  3    from gp.patient;

View created.

SQL> select * from patient_info;

SURNAME                                FORENAMES                          G DATE_OF_B
-------------------------------------  -------------------------------    - ---------
Gloria                                 Heyward                            F 12-OCT-43
Ian                                    Allen                             M 29-FEB-64
Mel                                    Andrews                           M 17-MAR-37
Ntina                                  Antoniou                          F 21-MAR-54
Audrey                                 Garland                           F 12-APR-50
Yolanda                                Baly                              F 25-JAN-39
Joanna                                 Bennett                           F 09-JAN-48
Mohand                                 Bougan                            M 20-JAN-65
Pat                                    Brady                             F 01-FEB-59
Dianne                                 Bullman                           F 27-APR-55
Jonathan                               Bramwell                          M 14-MAY-56

SURNAME                                FORENAMES                          G DATE_OF_B
-------------------------------------  -------------------------------    - ---------
Steve                                  Husson                            M 12-JUN-66
David                                  Bullman                           M 29-MAR-53
Kelly                                  Bullman                           F 13-JAN-83
Ashley                                 Bullman                           M 13-JAN-83
David                                  Carrington                        M 05-JUL-27
Beatrice                               Casey                             F 15-AUG-17
Linda                                  Chaplin                           F 19-SEP-53
Debbie                                 Creasey                           F 25-JAN-55
Ian                                    Matthews                          M 04-MAR-46
Richard                                Thompson                          M 19-FEB-46
Sandra                                 Denny                             F 18-MAY-48

SURNAME                                FORENAMES                          G DATE_OF_B
-------------------------------------  -------------------------------    - ---------
Steve                                  Miller                            M 07-OCT-40
Norma                                  Waterson                          F 22-JUN-42
Eliza                                  McCarthy                          F 31-JAN-67
Debbie                                 Cuthbert                          F 08-MAR-55
John                                   Cuthbert                          M 17-FEB-47
James                                  Cuthbert                          M 13-APR-87
Catherine                              Fergusson                         F 31-JUL-23
Brian                                  Foley                             M 30-JAN-68
Emma                                   Fraser                            F 31-JUL-37
Sydney                                 Fraser                            M 02-MAR-90
Margaret                               Phillipou                         F 16-MAY-43

SURNAME                                FORENAMES                          G DATE_OF_B
-------------------------------------  -------------------------------    - ---------
```

Lab4.2.2: Create a view that masks values in the column.

1) You need to create a view **doctor_info** based on the **GP** table that shows information from all columns, but for the gender it displays 'Male' instead of 'M' and 'Female' instead of 'F'

Complete the following SQL command and execute it.

CREATE OR REPLACE VIEW doctor_info AS

SELECT ...., DECODE(....) gender

```
FROM gp.gp;
```

2) Test your new view

```
SELECT * FROM doctor_info;
```

Question3: Provide the complete SQL command for the *doctor_info* view and the screen shot of the test result.

```
CREATE OR REPLACE VIEW doctor_info AS

SELECT BMA_NO,PRACTICE_POSTCODE,FORENAMES,SURNAME,
DECODE(GENDER,'M','Male','F','Female')GENDER

FROM gp.gp;
```

```
Oracle SQL*Plus
File  Edit  Search  Options  Help

SQL> CREATE OR REPLACE VIEW DOCTOR_INFO AS
  2  SELECT BMA_NO,PRACTICE_POSTCODE,FORENAMES
  3  ,SURNAME,DECODE(GENDER,'M','Male','F','Female')
  4  GENDER FROM GP.GP;

View created.

SQL> SELECT * FROM DOCTOR_INFO;

BMA_NO      PRACTICE_P FORENAMES       SURNAME          GENDER
----------  ---------- --------------- ---------------- ------
BM101-87    N8 8SU     Khan            Imran            Male
BM346-92    N8 8SU     Molby           Ian              Male
BM454-65    N8 8SU     Patel           Nina             Female
BM767-85    N8 8SU     Ross            Judith           Female
BM626-83    N8 8SU     Murray          Hayet            Female
BM939-59    N8 8SU     Campley         Susan            Female
BM888-68    N8 8SU     Nicolaou        Nicos            Male
BM092-77    N8 8SU     Patterson       Walter           Male

8 rows selected.
```

Lab 2.3.3: Create views that implement fine-grained access requirement: each doctor can see information only about his/her patients.

1) You need to create two views - one for the doctor Nina Patel and one for the doctor Walter Patterson. Each view must select information from **GP** table, **APPOINTMENT** table and **PATIENT** table. Each view has to show doctor's last name, patient last name, patient first name and patient appointment date.

a) Complete the following SQL command and execute it.

```
CREATE OR REPLACE view nina_patel AS

SELECT . . .
```

```
FROM gp.gp d, gp.appointment a, gp.patient p

WHERE . . .

AND . . .;
```

b) Complete the following SQL command and execute it.

```
CREATE OR REPLACE view walter_patterson AS

SELECT . . .

FROM gp.gp d, gp.appointment a, gp.patient p

WHERE . . .

AND . . .;
```

2) Test your new views.

```
SELECT * FROM nina_patel;

SELECT * FROM walter_patterson;
```

Question4: Provide the complete SQL command for the *nina_patel* view and the *walter_patterson* view as well as the screen shots of the test results.
a.)

```
CREATE OR REPLACE view nina_patel AS

SELECT d.forenames as
"doc_last_name",p.surname,p.forenames,a.date_time

FROM gp.gp d, gp.appointment a, gp.patient p

WHERE d.forenames='Patel' AND d.BMA_NO=a.BMA_NO

AND p.NHS_NO=a.NHS_NO;
```

```
Oracle SQL*Plus
File  Edit  Search  Options  Help

SQL> ed
Wrote file afiedt.buf

  1  CREATE OR REPLACE view nina_patel AS
  2  SELECT d.forenames as "doc_last_name",p.surname,p.forenames,a.date_time
  3  FROM gp.gp d, gp.appointment a, gp.patient p
  4  WHERE d.forenames='Patel'
  5  AND d.BMA_NO=a.BMA_NO
  6* AND p.NHS_NO=a.NHS_NO
SQL> /

View created.

SQL> select * from nina_patel;

doc_last_name              SURNAME               FORENAMES             DATE_TIME
-------------------------- --------------------- --------------------- ---------
Patel                      Debbie                Creasey               02-OCT-97
Patel                      Linda                 Chaplin               02-OCT-97
Patel                      Debbie                Creasey               03-OCT-97
Patel                      Eliza                 McCarthy              03-OCT-97
Patel                      Debbie                Cuthbert              03-OCT-97
Patel                      Beatrice              Casey                 03-OCT-97
Patel                      John                  Cuthbert              04-OCT-97
Patel                      Eliza                 McCarthy              04-OCT-97
Patel                      Eliza                 McCarthy              05-OCT-97
Patel                      Debbie                Cuthbert              05-OCT-97
Patel                      Beatrice              Casey                 05-OCT-97

doc_last_name              SURNAME               FORENAMES             DATE_TIME
-------------------------- --------------------- --------------------- ---------
Patel                      John                  Cuthbert              05-OCT-97
Patel                      Steve                 Miller                05-OCT-97
Patel                      Richard               Thompson              06-OCT-97
Patel                      Eliza                 McCarthy              06-OCT-97
Patel                      Richard               Thompson              06-OCT-97
Patel                      Eliza                 McCarthy              06-OCT-97
Patel                      Richard               Thompson              06-OCT-97

18 rows selected.
```

b.)

CREATE OR REPLACE view *walter_patterson* AS

SELECT d.forenames as
"doc_last_name",p.surname,p.forenames,a.date_time

FROM gp.gp d, gp.appointment a, gp.patient p

WHERE d.forenames='Patterson' AND d.BMA_NO=a.BMA_NO

AND p.NHS_NO=a.NHS_NO;

```
Oracle SQL*Plus
File  Edit  Search  Options  Help

 1  CREATE OR REPLACE view walter_patterson AS
 2  SELECT d.forenames as "doc_last_name",p.surname,p.forenames,a.date_time
 3  FROM gp.gp d, gp.appointment a, gp.patient p
 4  WHERE d.forenames='Patterson' AND d.BMA_NO=a.BMA_NO
 5* AND p.NHS_NO=a.NHS_NO
SQL> /

View created.

SQL> select * from walter_patterson;

doc_last_name                     SURNAME            FORENAMES                         DATE_TIME
--------------------------------  -----------------  --------------------------------  ---------
Patterson                         Claire             Tikly                             02-OCT-97
Patterson                         Nick               Osmond                            02-OCT-97
Patterson                         Doug               Walker                            03-OCT-97
Patterson                         Gerrie             Walker                            03-OCT-97
Patterson                         Wei                Li Fung                           03-OCT-97
Patterson                         Dave               Rubbish                           04-OCT-97
Patterson                         Gerrie             Walker                            04-OCT-97
Patterson                         Wei                Li Fung                           04-OCT-97
Patterson                         Theresa            Wilson                            04-OCT-97
Patterson                         Wei                Li Fung                           05-OCT-97
Patterson                         Dave               Spinks                            06-OCT-97

11 rows selected.
```

Question5: What are the limitations of using views for the implementing this requirement: each doctor can see information only about his/her patients? Explain.

By implementing this view, the doctor can see information only about his/her patients from the table. If that condition is removed, then it will result in the table displaying a Cartesian product of the records from all 3 tables. Also, if the view contains columns from more than one table, then data manipulation operations can't be performed on the view and if the table on which the view is created is dropped, then the view won't work and since views are database objects, it will occupy space.

2.4 LAB: Implementing Virtual private database

Oracle Virtual Private Database (VPD) enables us to create security policies to control database access at the row and column level. Essentially, VPD adds a dynamic WHERE clause to a SQL statement that is issued against the table, view, or synonym to which a VPD security policy was applied.

When a user directly or indirectly accesses a table, view, or synonym that is protected with a VPD policy, database dynamically modifies the SQL statement of the user. This modification creates a WHERE condition (called a predicate) returned by a function implementing the security policy. Database modifies the statement dynamically, transparently to the user, using any condition that can be expressed in or returned by a function. We can apply VPD policies to SELECT, INSERT, UPDATE, and DELETE statements.

In this laboratory project we will implement a small VPD system based on GP schema, which we have already used previously. In the Lab 4 we have implemented the fine-grained access in the database using database views. Now we will implement the fine-grained access through VPD and Application Context.

What Is an Application Context?

An application context is a set of name-value pairs that Oracle Database stores in memory. Think of an application context as a variable that holds information that is accessed during a database session.

In order to retrieve data from application context we will use the SYS_CONTEXT function, which returns the value of the parameter associated with the context namespace. We can use this function in both SQL and PL/SQL statements.

The SYS_CONTEXT function provides a default namespace, USERENV, which returns values about current session of the user logged on as well about some non-session related values such as database name, the database domain and server host. We can use SYS_CONTEXT to retrieve different types of information about a user, such as the user host computer ID, IP address, operating system user name, and so on.

For example, to retrieve the name of the host computer to which a client is connected, you can use the HOST parameter of USERENV as follows:

SELECT SYS_CONTEXT ('USERENV', 'HOST') FROM DUAL;

NOTE: By default all data stored in application context in UPPER case.
DUAL is a dummy table that doesn't contain any data but can be used in any SELECT for formatting purposes.

Objectives

At the end of this lab, we will be able to:

- Use the SYS_CONTEXT function to retrieve information on application context
- Implement VPD techniques to provide fine-grained access control
- Apply security policies and develop security functions

ERD of the GP schema:

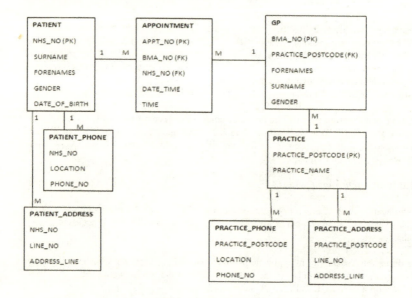

Lab 2.4.1: Investigate application context using SYS_CONTEXT function.

1) Retrieve values of the following USERENV parameters:

```
AUTHENTICATION_METHOD
CURRENT_SCHEMA
SESSION_USER
SESSION_USERID
HOST
```

Below command respectively is used to retrieve the value for the AUTHENTICATION_METHOD, CURRENT_SCHEMA, SESSION_USER, SESSION_USERID, and HOST as the USERENV parameter from SYS_CONTEXT and from DUAL.

```
SELECT SYS_CONTEXT ('USERENV', 'AUTHENTICATION_METHOD') FROM DUAL;

SELECT SYS_CONTEXT ('USERENV', 'CURRENT_SCHEMA') FROM DUAL;

SELECT SYS_CONTEXT ('USERENV', 'SESSION_USER') FROM DUAL;

SELECT SYS_CONTEXT ('USERENV', 'SESSION_USERID') FROM DUAL;

SELECT SYS_CONTEXT ('USERENV', 'HOST') FROM DUAL;
```

We will get the output for this command as:

PASSWORD

KD105

KD105

144

CMS_DOMAIN\CMSVDISEP020

a) Open SQL*plus and connect to yoda database as your primary yoda account.

To connect to SQL*plus use the following command:
CONNECT kd105/kd105@yoda;

b) Use SYS_CONTEXT function to retrieve necessary information. You can use the following example:

SELECT SYS_CONTEXT ('USERENV', 'AUTHENTICATION_METHOD') FROM DUAL;

We will the output as:
PASSWORD

NOTE: By default all data stored in application context in UPPER case.

Question1: Provide the complete SQL command **for each parameter listed above** and the screen shot of the result.

Below is the screenshot of parameters listed:

SQL> SELECT SYS_CONTEXT ('USERENV', 'HOST') FROM DUAL;

SYS_CONTEXT('USERENV','HOST')

CMS_DOMAIN\CMSVDISEP020

SQL> SELECT SYS_CONTEXT ('USERENV', 'AUTHENTICATION_METHOD') FROM DUAL;

SYS_CONTEXT('USERENV','AUTHENTICATION_METHOD')

PASSWORD

```
SQL> SELECT SYS_CONTEXT ('USERENV', 'CURRENT_SCHEMA') FROM DUAL;

SYS_CONTEXT('USERENV','CURRENT_SCHEMA')
----------------------------------------------------------------------------
KD105

SQL> SELECT SYS_CONTEXT ('USERENV', 'SESSION_USER') FROM DUAL;

SYS_CONTEXT('USERENV','SESSION_USER')
----------------------------------------------------------------------------
KD105


SQL> SELECT SYS_CONTEXT ('USERENV', 'SESSION_USERID') FROM DUAL;

SYS_CONTEXT('USERENV','SESSION_USERID')
----------------------------------------------------------------------------
144
```

Lab 2.4.2: Create VPD that implement fine-grained access requirement: each doctor can see information only about his/her patients in the APPOINTMENT table.

NOTE: As in the previous labs, everywhere in the lab assignment you need to replace reference 'XXXX' with your yoda database user name in upper case. For example if your yoda user name is abc12 then you must replace **XXXX** with **ABC12**.

In this lab we will use two doctors as an example - Nina Patel and Walter Patterson. In the Lab2 we've created two users: kd105_A and kd105_B user (where kd105 is yoda username).

You will assume that Nina Patel is kd105_A user and Walter Patterson is kd105_B user.

1) First, you need to create a copy of the GP.APPOINTMENT table in your own schema, so that you can test VPD without affecting the original schema:

*CREATE TABLE my_appointment as SELECT * FROM gp.appointment;*

Now you have my_appointment table that you own and therefore you have all privileges to this table.

2) Check how many appointments each doctor has. You can use their BMA numbers:

Nina Patel's BMA_NO is **BM454-65**

Walter Patterson's BMA_NO is **BM092-77.**

You can use the following code as a sample:

For Nina Patel:

*SQL> SELECT * FROM MY_APPOINTMENT WHERE BMA_NO=***'BM454-65';**

Write down the number of appointments for Nina Patel

Nina Patel has 18 appointments.

For Walter Patterson:

SQL> SELECT * FROM GP.APPOINTMENT WHERE BMA_NO='BM092-77';

Write down the number of appointments for Walter Patterson

Walter Patterson has 11 appointments.

3) You have to grant SELECT privilege on MY_APPOINTMENT table to your kd105_A user and kd105_B user.

To grant SELECT privilege on MY_APPOINTMENT table to the user kd105_A and kd105_B use the following command:

GRANT SELECT ON MY_APPOINTMENT TO KD105_A, KD105_B;

Question2: What SQL command do you need to execute to grant the SELECT privilege on your MY_APPOINTMENT table to your XXXX_A user and XXXX_B user?

Write down SQL command and execute it.

To grant SELECT privilege on MY_APPOINTMENT table to the user kd105_A and kd105_B use the following command:

GRANT SELECT ON MY_APPOINTMENT TO KD105_A, KD105_B;

5) Now you need to create a PL/SQL function (we will name it *RESTRICT_GP*) that will return an additional WHERE condition - the predicate. The function will check who is logged in at the moment by using an application context SESSION_USER: if the user is kd105_A is logged in (Nina Patel), then the predicate will be 'BMA_NO=''BM454-65''', so that her queries against kd105.MY_APPOINTMENT table will be appended automatically with the condition WHERE BMA_NO='BM454-65'.

If the user logged in is kd105_B (Walter Patterson) then the predicate will be 'BMA_NO=''BM092-77''', and if anybody else - then no predicate will be returned (the function returns NULL).

NOTE: The predicate is a string and therefore has to be included in single quotes, but inside the predicate the value BM454-65 is a string as well and therefore has to be included in single quotes as well. In situations like this when one single quoted expression has to be included into another single quoted expression, you must use <u>TWO SINGLE QUOTES</u> (NOT double quotes!!) for the inside expression:

'BMA_NO=''BM454-65'' '

You can use the following PL/SQL code to create function *RESTRICT_GP:*

```
CREATE OR REPLACE FUNCTION RESTRICT_GP

(P_SCHEMA IN VARCHAR2, P_OBJECT IN VARCHAR2)

RETURN VARCHAR2

AS

BEGIN

  IF SYS_CONTEXT('USERENV', 'SESSION_USER')='XXXX_A'

    THEN    RETURN 'BMA_NO=''BM454-65''';

  ELSIF SYS_CONTEXT('USERENV', 'SESSION_USER')='XXXX_B'

    THEN    RETURN 'BMA_NO=''BM092-77''';

  ELSE RETURN NULL;

  END IF;

END;

/
```

> Replace XXXX with your username in UPPER CASE

Note: These are TWO SINGLE QOUTES and THREE SINGLE QUOTES!!!

NOTE: Make sure function RESTRICT_GP is created successfully.

If you receive a feedback message *Warning: Function created with compilation errors,* it means that the function cannot be used until you fix all errors. To get information about your errors use following command:

SHOW errors

Try to fix your errors and re-create the function until you receive a feedback message:

Function created.

6) You need to create a security policy and attach it to your *MY_APPOINTMENT* table. This security policy would use your function *RESTRICT_GP* and dynamically modify the SQL statement of the user by adding the predicate and therefore will provide **a VPD** functionality. In order to add policy to the table you need to use **DBMS_RLS** PL/SQL package, which is provided with the database.

The DBMS_RLS package contains procedures and functions that provide the interface to add, drop or enable security policies. **ADD_POLICY** procedure adds a fine-grained access control policy to a table, view, or synonym.

You can use the following code with yoda username in UPPER CASE.

NOTE: All string values in the code are in **UPPER CASE.**

> Replace XXXX with your
> username in UPPER CASE

```
BEGIN

DBMS_RLS.ADD_POLICY(

OBJECT_SCHEMA => 'XXXX',

OBJECT_NAME => 'MY_APPOINTMENT',

POLICY_NAME => 'GPONLY',

FUNCTION_SCHEMA => 'XXXX',

POLICY_FUNCTION => 'RESTRICT_GP'

);

END;

/
```

Note: Make sure the PL/SQL code executed successfully. You should get message

PL/SQL procedure successfully completed.

Lab 2.4.3: Test your VPD as Nina Patel and as Walter Patterson.

1) Test VPD for Nina Patel.

    a) Connect to yoda as kd105_A user (Nina Patel)

    b) Select data from kd105.MY_APPOINTMENT table.

NOTE: You have to use prefix kd105 in front of the table name because the user kd105_A doesn't own the table my_appontment and therefore he has to prefix the name of the owner as kd105.MY_APPOINTMENT

    *SQL> SELECT * FROM kd105.MY_APPOINTMENT;*

Question3: How many records did you get? Are these appointments for Nina Patel? (Compare with your record from Lab5.2 step 2). Provide a screen-shot of the result for Nina Patel and explain it.

By querying the appointments of Nina Patel using command:

*SELECT * FROM kd105.MY_APPOINTMENT;*

We will get 18 appointments as shown in the screenshot below.

```
SQL> CONNECT KD105_A/connect1@yoda;
Connected.
SQL> select * from kd105.MY_APPOINTMENT;

    APPT_NO BMA_NO            NHS_NO                  DATE_TIME  TIME
----------- ----------------  ----------------------  ---------- ------
          6 BM454-65          FGAH529                 02-OCT-97 10:00
          9 BM454-65          FTAH428                 02-OCT-97 10:30
         28 BM454-65          FGAH529                 03-OCT-97 10:00
         30 BM454-65          FKAJ125                 03-OCT-97 10:30
         31 BM454-65          FMAI226                 03-OCT-97 11:00
         32 BM454-65          FNAH327                 03-OCT-97 11:30
         52 BM454-65          MJAK327                 04-OCT-97 10:00
         63 BM454-65          FKAJ125                 04-OCT-97 10:30
         83 BM454-65          FKAJ125                 05-OCT-97 10:00
         84 BM454-65          FMAI226                 05-OCT-97 10:30
         86 BM454-65          FNAH327                 05-OCT-97 11:00

    APPT_NO BMA_NO            NHS_NO                  DATE_TIME  TIME
----------- ----------------  ----------------------  ---------- ------
         95 BM454-65          MJAK327                 05-OCT-97 11:30
         96 BM454-65          MLAH923                 05-OCT-97 12:00
         98 BM454-65          MPAY721                 06-OCT-97 10:00
        107 BM454-65          FKAJ125                 06-OCT-97 10:30
        110 BM454-65          MPAY721                 06-OCT-97 11:00
        114 BM454-65          FKAJ125                 06-OCT-97 11:30
        116 BM454-65          MPAY721                 06-OCT-97 12:00

18 rows selected.
```

2) Test VPD for Walter Patterson.

    a) Connect to yoda as XXXX_B user (Walter Patterson)

    b) Select data from XXXX.APPOINTMENT table.

```
SQL> SELECT * FROM kd105.MY_APPOINTMENT;
```

Question4: Provide a screen-shot of the result for Walter Patterson and explain it.

By querying the appointments of Walter Patterson using command:

*SELECT * FROM kd105.MY_APPOINTMENT;*

We will get 11 appointments as shown in the screenshot below.

```
SQL> CONNECT KD105_B/connect2@yoda;
Connected.
SQL> select * from kd105.my_appointment;

  APPT_NO BMA_NO              NHS_NO                   DATE_TIME TIME
---------- -------------      -----------------       --------- -----
       13 BM092-77            FXAU201                 02-OCT-97 10:00
       17 BM092-77            MEAT212                 02-OCT-97 10:30
       35 BM092-77            MDAH247                 03-OCT-97 10:00
       44 BM092-77            FFAT238                 03-OCT-97 10:30
       47 BM092-77            FTA0266                 03-OCT-97 11:00
       57 BM092-77            MWAE274                 04-OCT-97 10:00
       60 BM092-77            FFAT238                 04-OCT-97 10:30
       65 BM092-77            FTA0266                 04-OCT-97 11:00
       66 BM092-77            FTAT254                 04-OCT-97 11:30
       87 BM092-77            FTA0266                 05-OCT-97 10:00
      101 BM092-77            MSAF294                 06-OCT-97 11:00

11 rows selected.
```

NOTE: If you policy doesn't work and we need to drop it and re-create it .

In order to drop the policy, connect as your primary yoda user and use the following code:

```
BEGIN
    DBMS_RLS.DROP_POLICY(
    OBJECT_SCHEMA => 'XXXX',        (Where XXXX is your yoda USERNAME in
UPPER CASE)      OBJECT_NAME => 'APPOINTMENT',
                 POLICY_NAME => 'GPONLY');
                        END;
        /
```

Question5: In the Lab4 you have implemented the fine-grained access for Nina Patel and Walter Patterson using database views and in the current Lab you used VPD.

Compare and contrast both methods; include advantages and disadvantages of each methods as well as your evaluation of both.

The choice of creating VPD or to use the views depends on the security requirements and policy.

Advantages, disadvantages of using VPD vs views:

Views can just hides columns, hides rows, masks data and aggregates data. Mainly in views data manipulation is difficult, it occupies space in the database, if the base table changes the view might become invalid and multiple views are required. Even though it can provide non redundant data at the request times it has limited updatability. However using VPD provides applying of fine grained access control policy; it enforces the business rules to limit row access, it provides high performance, different access rules to different sql statements and group policies.

VPD defines policies as static, context sensitive or dynamic and the policies are stored in the memory so it provides high performance. VPD policy just needs to be defined once.

2.5 LAB: Churchill secondary school database security policy

2.5.1 Database Security policy:

Confidentiality, integrity and availability play an important role in the creation of the database security policy and in securing the data for all organizations.

Users in Churchill secondary school can be classified as teachers, teaching assistants, education psychologist, administrative staff, head and vice head teacher.

Head and vice head is responsible for providing privileges to all users in college.

Authentication:

Authentication for the database is very important, otherwise there will be misuse of data if unauthorized access to database is provided.

Authentication can be implemented by creating users, creating & assigning profiles to the users.

Profiles must be defined to restrict the number of failure attempts, complexity of password and the like.

Authorization:

By using authorization we can define roles and privileges to users for allowing or restricting access to users.

Authorization can be implemented by grant the privileges to the users, no access must be provided beyond the limit to the users.

Teaching assistant have read only access to the teaching materials from the teacher they are allocated.

Teachers have full access to the teaching materials.

Head and vice head have full access to the whole Churchill database.

Fine grained access:

Fine grained access to the users can be provided to the users by allowing and restricting access to the authorized and particular ueers for a particular content.

Fine grained access can be provided in the database by using views and virtual private database.

Virtual private database can provide row level and column level security. However views just masks the data in the database.

Auditing:

Auditing is the evaluation of the user actions in the database.

Auditing will generally be carried out by the security personnels who have administrative access to the database.

Auditing can be done by implementing effective security policies, denying the unauthorized access to the database, monitoring the logs of failure, and monitoring the behaviour of the users.

2.5.2 Database Security policy implementation: (profiles, roles, permissions, privileges, VPD, Views)

As per the specification there are 80 students, 10 teachers, 20 teaching assistants, 5 educational psychologists, 5 administrative staff, 1 head and 1 vice head teacher.

Security policy for the database must be implemented using SQL*PLUS:

1) First, create a database called Churchill.

2) Next we must create the table pupil_prof, employees, departments and Teach_mat.

To create table pupil_prof, employees, departments, and Teach_mat use CREATE TABLE command as follows:

Ex:

CREATE TABLE pupil_prof (s_id NUMBER(10), S_fname VARCHAR2(30), S_lname VARCHAR2(30), fa_name VARCHAR2(30), DOB DATE, Add VARCHAR2(40), Contact_number NUMBER (15), sub_marks VARCHAR2(50));

CREATE TABLE employees (e_id NUMBER(10), e_fname VARCHAR2(30), e_lname VARCHAR2(30), DOB DATE, Add VARCHAR2(40), Qualifications VARCHAR(50), Designation VARCHAR2(20), D_id VARCHAR2(30), Sub_id VARCHAR2(30));

CREATE TABLE department (d_id NUMBER(5), d_name VARCHAR2(30));

CREATE TABLE Teach_mat (T_id NUMBER(5), T_Name VARCHAR2(30), d_id NUMBER (5), e_id NUMBER(10), t_information VARCHAR2(100));

3) Insert the records or data into these tables using INSERT command as shown below:

Ex:

INSERT INTO pupil_prof (1, 'Avril', 'Lavigne' Jean Claude Lavigne', '27-Sep-1984', ' '21 high street cannada ontario', '07404289300');

In the same way as shown in the example insert records to all the tables of employees, departments, subjects, Teach_mat including pupil_prof.

4) Now we need to users by using CREATE USER command as shown below:

Ex:

Considering Nina patel as teacher we have inserted into the employees table in the step above and Nina patel has an employee id as 4011000100

CREATE USER np100 IDENTIFIED BY abcd123;

In the same way as shown in example create users for all teachers, teaching assistants, educational psychologists, managers and administrative staff. Use different default password for different roles of users.

5) GRANT CREATE SESSION privilege for all users.

6) Now first create profiles for the users.

We need 5 profiles namely teachers_prof, teaching_assistants_prof, edu_psycho_prof, administrators_prof, and managers_prof.

Profiles can be created by using command shown in example:

Ex:

CREATE PROFILE teachers_prof

LIMIT FAILED_LOGIN_ATTEMPTS 2

PASSWORD_LOCK_TIME 1

PASSWORD_LIFE_TIME_180

PASSWORD_REUSE_TIME 2

PASSWORD_REUSE_MAX UNLIMITED;

In the same way create the remaining profiles.

7) Now create the 5 roles namely teachers, teaching_assistants, edu_psycho, admin, managers using CREATE ROLE command

Ex:

CREATE ROLE teachers;

In the same way creates all the roles.

8) Assign profile for the users using the command shown below:

Ex:

ALTER USER np100 PROFILE teachers_prof;

In the same way assign profile for teachers, teaching assistants, educational psychologists, managers and administrative staff with teachers_prof, teaching_assistants_prof, edu_psycho_prof, administrators_prof, and managers_prof respectively.

9) Now grant the roles necessary privileges.

It can granted as using GRANT command shown below:

Ex:

As Head and vice head teacher manages the school and they must have full access to all information in the school's database.

We need to grant the permission for the manager role:

GRANT ALL on pupil_prof, employees, departments, Teach_mat to manager;

In the same way we will grant appropriate permissions to all roles.

10) Now grant the roles to all the users appropriately using GRANT command as shown below.

Ex:

GRANT teachers to teacher1, teacher2, teacher3, teacher4, teacher5, teacher6, teacher7, teacher8, teacher9, teacher10;

Here teacher1, ... teacher10 are the teacher assigned usernames.

For Nina patel if we want to grant role as teacher we use:

GRANT teachers to np100;

11) Implement virtual private database using the following example below:

EX:

CREATE OR REPLACE FUNCTION RESTRICT_GENERAL

(P_SCHEMA IN VARCHAR2, P_OBJECT IN VARCHAR2)

RETURN VARCHAR2

AS

BEGIN

> **Replace XXXX with username in UPPER CASE**

IF SYS_CONTEXT('USERENV', 'SESSION_USER')='XXXX'

THEN   RETURN 'BMA_NO="BM454-65"';

ELSIF SYS_CONTEXT('USERENV', 'SESSION_USER')='XXXX'

THEN   RETURN 'XXX_NO="YYY"';

ELSE RETURN NULL;

END IF;

END;

Here YYY can be implemented to the teachers who only need access to the pupil's profile for which they are handling the class.

In the same way, it is also applicable to teaching assistants who need the access only to the teaching materials from their assigned teacher. However we need to provide SELECT ON privilege only to the teaching assistants as they need to have read only access.

    12) Add security policy to the tables by using a creating a restrict function as explained in the example below:

Ex:

BEGIN

DBMS_RLS.ADD_POLICY(

OBJECT_SCHEMA => 'XXXX',

OBJECT_NAME => ABCD',

POLICY_NAME => 'TEACHERS',

FUNCTION_SCHEMA => 'XXXX',

POLICY_FUNCTION => 'RESTRICT_GENERAL'

);

END;

/

Replace XXXX usernam in UPPER CASE

    13) Grant permissions to the tables appropriately using GRANT command.

To Grant read only access use GRANT SELECT ON command.

    14) Test the permissions and privileges by logging in to one user in each role.

Fine-grained access can be provided by using both views and virtual private database. However, implementing Virtual private database provides good security.

To create fine-grained access by views we have to implement views after 10th step by using CREATE OR REPLACE VIEW command.

2.5.3 Final report: -

Database security is one of the most critical parts of the security in all organizations. If the database security policy is not implemented correctly in the organization, there are high chances of loss of data. Organizations cannot afford to lose their business data. So security policies must be implemented correctly and must be tested.

In this Part 2 coursework, We learnt creating tables, inserting records, creating profiles, creating roles, assigning profiles, assigning roles, providing privileges, permissions, views, and virtual private database.

We created a database security policy for the Churchill secondary school and explained the steps for the implementation of the security policy using profiles, roles, permissions, privileges, virtual private database and views.

References

Agee. Sara. (2006) *Bit Depth, colors and Digital photos.* [Online] Available: http://www.sciencebuddies.org/science-fair-projects/project_ideas/Photo_p009.shtml. Last accessed 13th Dec 2011.

Emeryville, Calif (2007) Mcgraw hill/Osborne London, McGraw hill distributor.

Haynes. Clives R. *Bit Depth and estimating file size.* [Online] Available: http://www.crhfoto.co.uk/crh/bitandfile.htm. Last accessed 13th Dec 2011.

Kessler. C Gary. (2001) *Steganography: Hiding data within data.* [Online] Available: http://www.garykessler.net/library/steganography.html. Last accessed 13th Dec 2011.

Exploring pixels and colors. [Online] Available: http://www.shortcourses.com/sensors/sensors1-18.html. Last accessed 13th Dec 2011.

How to remove watermark from an image or picture. [Online] Available: http://www.instantfundas.com/2010/04/how-to-remove-watermark-from-image-or.html. Last accessed 13th Dec 2011.

Oracle Database Security Guide 11g Release1 (11.1)part number B28531-14. [Online] Available: http://docs.oracle.com/cd/B28359_01/network.111/b28531/users.htm. Last accessed 13th Dec 2011.

Pixel color Depth or bits per pixel in digital photos. [Online] Available: http://www.streetdirectory.com/travel_guide/104339/photography/pixel_color_depth_or_bits _per_pixel_in_digital_photos.html. Last accessed 13th Dec 2011.

YOUR KNOWLEDGE HAS VALUE